Munching

Poems About Eating

Munching

Poems About Eating

Selected by Lee Bennett Hopkins

Illustrations by Nelle Davis

Little, Brown and Company
Boston   Toronto

Second Printing

Library of Congress Cataloging-in-Publication Data

Main entry under title:
Munching: poems about eating.
    Includes index.
    Summary: A collection of poems centering on the plea-
sures of food by a variety of English and American poets.
    1. Food—Juvenile poetry.   2. Children's poetry, Ameri-
can.   3. Children's poetry, English.   4. American
poetry—20th century.   5. English poetry—19th century.
[1. Food-Poetry.   2. American poetry—Collections.
3. English poetry—Collections]   I. Hopkins, Lee
Bennett.   II. Davis, Nelle, ill.
PS595.F65M86 1985   811'.008'0355   85-13037
ISBN 0-316-37269-2 (lib. bdg.)

Acknowledgments

The Crown Publishing Group for the extract reprinted from *Munch* by Alexandra Wallner. Copyright
© 1976 by Alexandra Wallner. Used by permission of Crown Publishers, Inc.

Curtis Brown, Ltd. for "Get 'Em Here" by Lee Bennett Hopkins. Copyright © 1970 by Lee Bennett
Hopkins; "Question" by Lee Bennett Hopkins. Copyright © 1974 by Lee Bennett Hopkins; "Artichoke"
by Maxine W. Kumin. Copyright © 1962 by Maxine W. Kumin. All reprinted by permission of Curtis
Brown, Ltd.

Ivy O. Eastwick for "Apple-Pie." Used by permission of the author, who controls all rights.

Charles J. Egita for "Fruited Rainbow." Used by permission of the author, who controls all rights.

Cynthia B. Francis for "Popsicles." Used by permission of the author, who controls all rights.

Harper & Row, Publishers, Inc. for "Sunny-Side-Up" from *Egg Thoughts and Other Frances Songs* by
Russell Hoban. Text Copyright © 1964, 1972 by Russell Hoban. Reprinted by permission of Harper &
Row, Publishers, Inc.

Continued on page 46

Published simultaneously in Canada
by Little, Brown & Company (Canada) Limited

Printed in the U.S.A.

For Don Marion Paradise—
who enjoys munching ever so much!

LBH

Contents

From
The Clean Platter
Ogden Nash

Bring salad or sausage or scone,
A berry or even a beet,
Bring an oyster, an egg, or a bone,
As long as it's something to eat.
If it's food,
It's food;
Never mind what kind of food.
Through thick and through thin
I am constantly in
The mood
For food.

Spaghetti! Spaghetti!

Jack Prelutsky

Spaghetti! spaghetti!
you're wonderful stuff,
I love you, spaghetti,
I can't get enough.
You're covered with sauce
and you're sprinkled with cheese,
spaghetti! spaghetti!
oh, give me some please.

Spaghetti! spaghetti!
piled high in a mound,
you wiggle, you wriggle,
you squiggle around.
There's slurpy spaghetti
all over my plate,
spaghetti! spaghetti!
I think you are great.

Spaghetti! spaghetti!
I love you a lot,
you're slishy, you're sloshy,
delicious and hot.
I gobble you down
oh, I can't get enough,
spaghetti! spaghetti!
you're wonderful stuff.

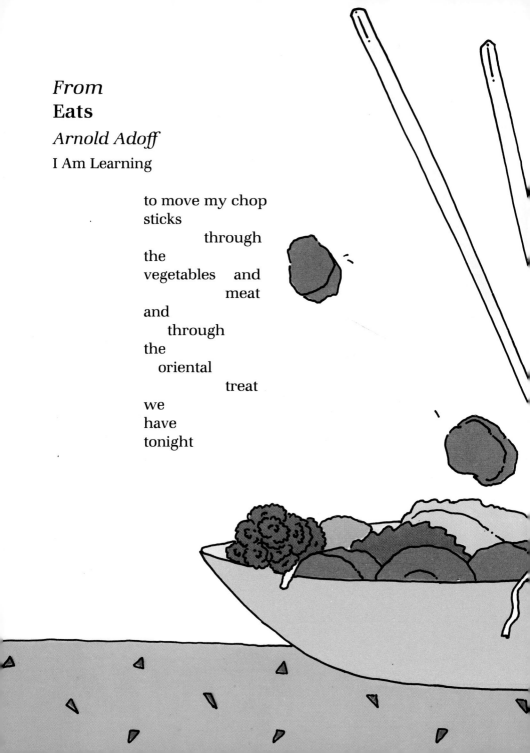

From
Eats
Arnold Adoff
I Am Learning

to move my chop
sticks
           through
the
vegetables   and
                meat
and
      through
the
    oriental
                treat
we
have
tonight

but   in
between
    my
    smiles
    and
        bites
            i
            write
            a
            message
                in
                    the
            sweet
                    and
            sour
            pork

            i
            need
            a
                fork

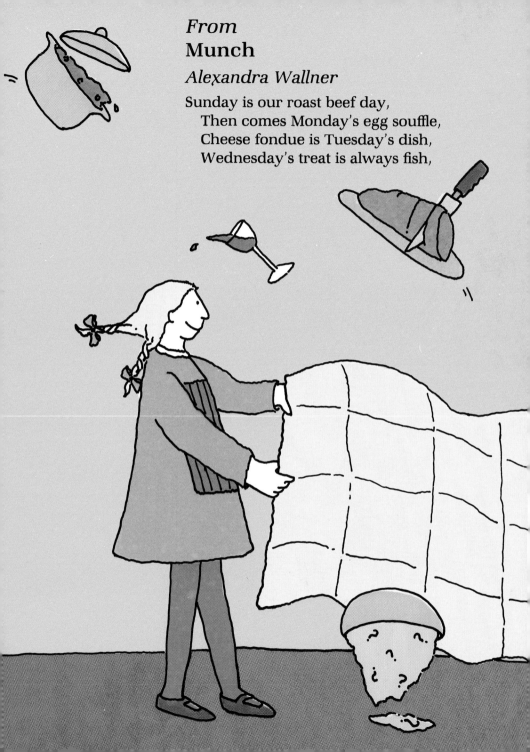

From
Munch

Alexandra Wallner

Sunday is our roast beef day,
    Then comes Monday's egg souffle,
    Cheese fondue is Tuesday's dish,
    Wednesday's treat is always fish,

Then comes Thursday's fricassee,
Friday's is a mystery,
And on Saturday we munch,
Leftover stews by the bunch.

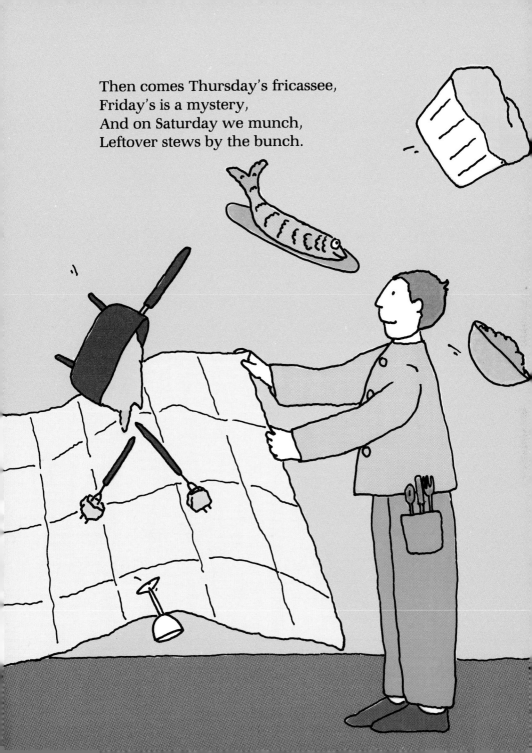

Sad Sweet Story

Norah Smaridge

Eat up your carrots and drink up your milk;
You'll have pearly-white teeth and a skin smooth as silk!
Eat too much candy, you'll end up instead
With a nutcracker jaw and no teeth in your head.

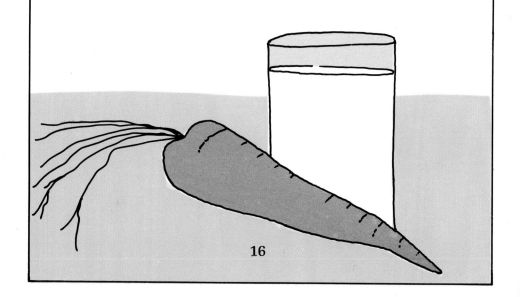

16

At the Table

Constance Andrea Keremes

Milk and cookies after school
    makes homework fun to do.

I   dunk

        subtract

                and take a bite

        and carry   over two.

Surprise

Margaret Hillert

I tip my glass to take a drink.
It goes down in a flash.
And when I've finished every drop,
I wear a milk mustache.

Question

Lee Bennett Hopkins

If cookies come in boxes
    And tuna comes in cans
And the butcher bakes our roast beef
    And wraps it in Saran

If most cakes come from bakeries
    And doughnuts from the store
I often sit and wonder
    What our kitchen oven's for?

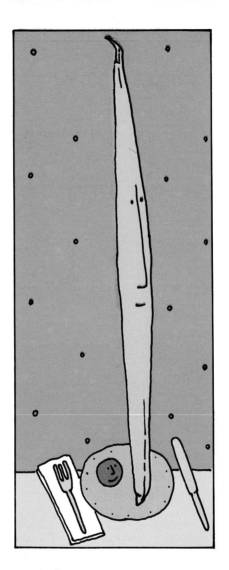

Limerick

Edward Lear

There was an Old Person of Dean
Who dined on one Pea, and one Bean;
    For he said, "More than that
    Would make me too fat,"
That cautious Old Person of Dean.

Sunny-Side-Up

Russell Hoban

With their yolks and whites all runny
They are looking at me funny.

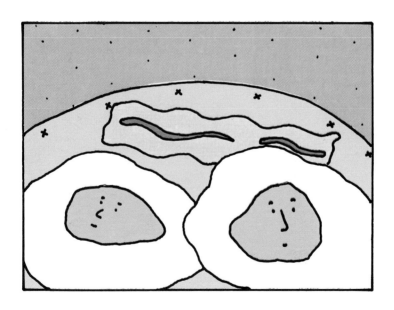

Turtle Soup

Lewis Carroll

Beautiful Soup, so rich and green,
Waiting in a hot tureen!
Who for such dainties would not stoop?
Soup of the evening, beautiful Soup!
Soup of the evening, beautiful Soup!
    Beau —— ootiful Soo —— oop!
    Beau —— ootiful Soo —— oop!
Soo —— oop of the e —— e —— evening,
    Beautiful, beautiful Soup!

Beautiful Soup! Who cares for fish,
Game, or any other dish?
Who would not give all else for two p
ennyworth only of beautiful Soup?
Pennyworth only of beautiful Soup?
    Beau —— ootiful Soo —— oop!
    Beau —— ootiful Soo —— oop!
Soo —— oop of the e —— e —— evening,
    Beautiful, beauti —— FUL SOUP!

Artichoke

Maxine W. Kumin

An artichoke
is a sort of joke
with layers of petals to peel,
like a box inside
of a box this wide
in a box in a box with a seal.

It's kind of a game
without any name
to nibble your way to the center.
Each petal you pull
tastes wonderful
till you get to the feathery splinter.

Well, you don't eat that,
you can bet your hat,
but under its thistly cloak
is the sweetest bite
for your appetite:
the heart of the artichoke.

Why

Prince Redcloud

We zoomed
to the moon
in just
a few years.

Why can't
we grow
onions
and
leave
out
the tears?

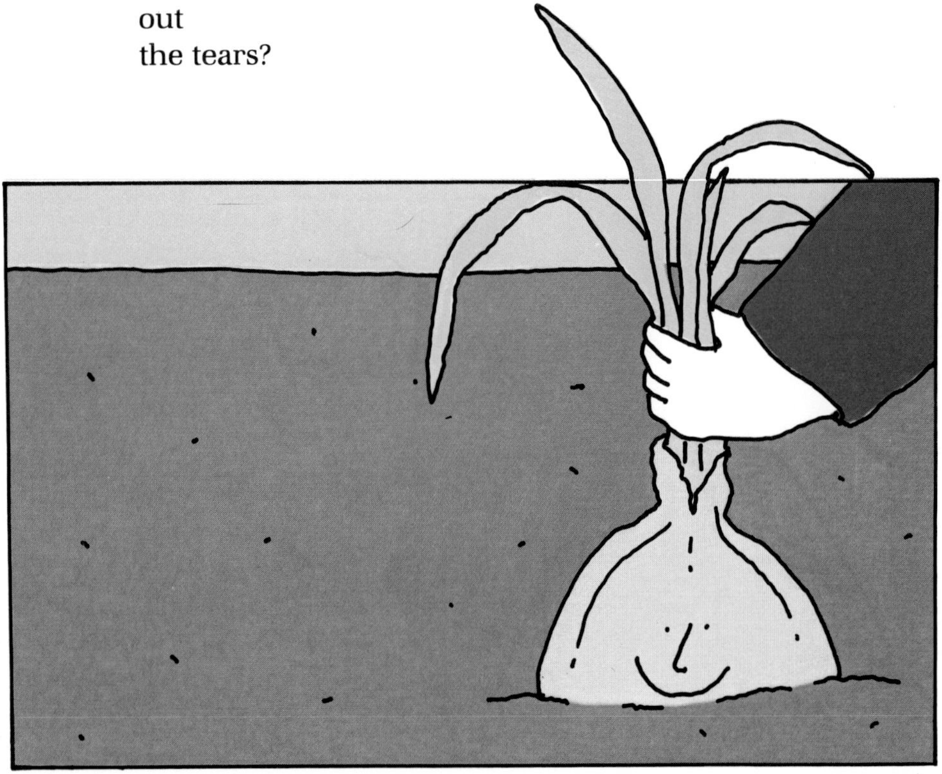

Drink a Garden

Kathy Mandry

Pour yourself a glass
of tomato juice.
Wash a small stalk of celery,
one red radish,
and the tip of a carrot.
Sprinkle a little salt
in the juice.
Take a sip, eat some radish.
Take another sip, eat some carrot.
Take another sip, eat some celery.
Keep going until it's all gone.
If you find the gardener's tools
at the bottom, give them back.

Get 'Em Here

Lee Bennett Hopkins

"Hot dogs with sauerkraut
Cold drinks here!
Hot dogs with sauerkraut
Get 'em here!
Hot dogs with sauerkraut
Cold drinks here!"

Shouts the man as he rolls the city's smallest
   store
All tucked neatly under a huge, blue- and-
   orange-striped umbrella.

The Pizza

Ogden Nash

Look at itsy-bitsy Mitzi!
See her figure slim and ritzy!
She eatsa
Pizza!
Greedy Mitzi!
She no longer itsy-bitsy!

The Perfect Turkey Sandwich

Steven Kroll

Is my craving so outlandish
For the perfect turkey sandwich?
All white meat sliced sweet and thin
Mayonnaise to soak it in
Crispy lettuce for the flavor
Well spread butter for its savor
Salt and pepper now, to taste
There won't be a crumb to waste
Sometimes in my sleep I sigh
Turkey sandwich please on rye.

Cookout Night

Dorothy Aldis

Paper cups and paper plates.
Pickles in a pickle jar.
Popcorn in a crackly bag.
Salt and pepper?
Here they are.

Paper napkins! Who forgot?
"I didn't, you did."
"I did *not.*
Besides what difference does it make?
Look at all the grass around
For wiping hands and faces on. . . ."

Nothing's ever impolite:
Not outdoors on cookout night.

Fruited Rainbow

Charles J. Egita

Fruits of orange, yellow, red,
Piled on a lettuce bed.

Sprinkled on top is coconut-snow.
O! What a bowl of rainbow-glow.

Popsicles

Cynthia B. Francis

Popsicles give cool wet kisses
To hot dry lips
On a beautiful summer day.

Bananas and Cream

David McCord

Bananas and cream,
Bananas and cream:
All we could say was
Bananas and cream.

We couldn't say fruit,
We wouldn't say cow,
We didn't say sugar —
We don't say it now.

Bananas and cream,
Bananas and cream,
All we could shout was
Bananas and cream.

We didn't say why,
We didn't say how;
We forgot it was fruit,
We forgot the old cow;
We *never* said sugar,
We only said *WOW!*

Bananas and cream,
Bananas and cream;
All that we want is
Bananas and cream!

We didn't say dish,
We didn't say spoon;
We said not tomorrow,
But NOW and HOW SOON

Bananas and cream,
Bananas and cream?
We yelled for bananas,
Bananas and scream!

Apple-Pie

Ivy O. Eastwick

I simply do not know why I
should be so fond of apple-pie.

And when I'm offered it with cheese
or cream, I always say: "Yes, please."

And no one has to ask me twice
I'll ALWAYS take a second slice.

Cake

David McCord

Take cake: a very easy rhyme for bake.
Take icing, which will always rhyme with slicing.
Take filling. Careful now — it rhymes with spilling.
Take crumbs: just as you take them, someone comes.
Take off! That's what you do. For sticky fingers
The rhyme is in the chocolate stain that lingers.

Index of Titles, Authors, and First Lines